# HOW TO PRAY

JIM KIBLER

ISBN: 1983741957
ISBN 13: 9781983741951
Library of Congress Control Number: 2018900786
CreateSpace Independent Publishing Platform
North Charleston, South Carolina

# ACKNOWLEDGEMENTS

Mary Kibler, my wife and ministry partner for her suggestions, editing, support and prayers.

Jean Johnson for her suggestions, editing, support and prayers.

Our wonderful church family and partners for their prayers and support.

All Scripture quotations are from the King James Version or Paraphrased.

# CONTENTS

# INTRODUCTION

Mary and I were recently in a Christian Book Store and I happen to see a book on prayer. I opened it up and saw where the author, who leads a very large prayer organization, make a statement that there is no magical formula or guarantee for getting God to answer prayers.

I showed the book to Mary and she said, "Well then, why bother praying." I thought to myself, hasn't this man even read the Bible.

On the way home I said "There are actually very few people who know how to pray and get results."

Another man, who was an expert on prayer and who also led a huge prayer organization of his own, had major health problems for several years. Every time he entered the hospital he would mobilize the prayer warriors and people would comment "Prayers going up." Bless his heart. The last time he mobilized the prayer warriors, he died. None of his "Prayer warriors" knew how to pray and get him healed. Apparently, he did not really know how to pray after all.

## UNANSWERED PRAYER IS NEVER GOD'S FAULT.

If you are not getting results when you pray, then something is wrong! Chances are very good that you are not praying correctly. I have heard people say that there is no wrong way to pray. That is not true. You can always tell when someone knows how to pray, because they get RESULTS.

If you are not getting results when you pray it is because you are not praying the right way and it's time to do something different. Prayers are supposed to be answered every time and that is what we should expect.

## GOD DOES NOT PICK OUT PRAYERS TO ANSWER

Many people believe that prayer is a hit or miss proposition. They believe that sometimes God says yes, sometimes God says no and sometimes God says maybe so. Wrong again! They pray and sometimes even get all of their friends to pray for them and hope that God will take a liking to at least one person's prayer on their behalf.

Most people never expect to get results when they pray. If that's the case, then prayer for them is a waste of time. The bottom line is that if you are not expecting results, then there is no need to pray.

## EXPECT YOUR PRAYERS TO BE ANSWERED

If you are getting no results, when you pray, find out what the reason is. Don't just assume that God has said no. God almost never says no.

The truth of the matter is, you can actually expect God to answer each and every prayer. If you learn how to pray the right way you will be amazed by the results.

It is my objective in writing this book, that after reading it, you will be able to pray about anything you want or need and quickly receive it from God.

# THE MOST IMPORTANT PRAYER

The most important prayer you will ever pray, is the prayer to receive Jesus as your Lord and Savior. If you have never prayed this prayer for salvation just pray it out loud now, mean it in your heart and you will be saved and will spend eternity in heaven.

Pray: Heavenly Father, I repent of my sins. I believe Jesus rose from the dead after shedding His Blood for my salvation. I ask you now, Lord Jesus, please come into my heart and be my Savior and I will serve you for all of eternity. Amen.

# WHAT PRAYER IS

Prayer is communication with God, or in the most basic terms, talking to God, person to person. It is the way of communicating our thoughts, needs and desires to God. Prayer is also an act. In Luke 11:1 the Bible tells us that Jesus finished praying, which means that prayer is an act, something you start and finish.

- Prayer is not trying to get God's attention.

- Prayer is not trying to get God to do something.

- Prayer is a method by which we receive what God has already provided for us.

- Prayer is a way for us to tell God how much we love Him.

- Prayer is so powerful that all it takes is one prayer to receive your eternal salvation.

## PRAYERS ARE A MEMORIAL BEFORE GOD

**Acts 10:1-4 There was a certain man in Caesarea called Cornelius, a centurion of the band called the Italian band,**

**2 A devout man, and one that feared God with all his house, which gave much alms to the people, and prayed to God always.**

**3 He saw in a vision about the ninth hour of the day, an angel of God coming in to him, and saying unto him, Cornelius.**

**4 And when he looked on him, he was afraid, and said, what is it, Lord? And he said unto him, your prayers and your alms are come up as a memorial before God.**

A memorial is something used to remember a person and apparently, God remembers you by your prayers which have come up, all the way to Heaven.

## GOD SAVES YOUR PRAYERS

**Revelation 5:8 And when he had taken the book, the four beasts and four and twenty elders fell down before the Lamb, having every one of them harps, and golden vases full of incense, which are the prayers of saints.**

To me, this verse is overwhelming. God actually saves your prayers in golden vases. Can you imagine this, that the Lord God, who holds the entire universe in the palm of His Hand, loves you so much that He keeps your prayers on file in a golden vase? I believe the most beautiful sound to God is the sound of your voice. How many of your prayers does God have on file in golden vases?

## GOD ALWAYS HEARS YOUR PRAYERS

**Psalm 34:15 The eyes of the LORD are upon the righteous, and his ears are open unto their cry.**

**Psalm 6:9 The LORD hath heard my supplication; the LORD will receive my prayer.**



DAN 10:12, 13 GOD HEARD DANIEL'S PRAYER THE VERY FIRST DAY.

God hears every prayer. He delights when we turn our cares over to Him and ask for help.

## PRAY TO THE FATHER

**John 16:23 And in that day, you shall ask me nothing. Verily, verily, I say unto you, whatsoever you shall ask the Father in my Name, he will give it you.**

Jesus is our Mediator, Intercessor, Advocate, and Lord. It is never recorded in the Bible that Jesus ever said, that people are to pray to Him. We are told by Jesus, to Pray to the Father, in the Name of Jesus.

When you pray to the Father, in the name of Jesus, your prayer becomes a legal document.

## GIVE YOUR CARES TO GOD

**Psalm 55:22 Cast your burden upon the LORD, and he shall sustain thee: he shall never suffer the righteous to be moved.**

When you give your burden to the Lord, LET HIM HAVE IT! Stop taking it back. Many people try to give their burdens to the Lord and then keep struggling with them. Once you ask the Lord to take care of a situation that is overwhelming you, step back and allow him to fix it. He will do just that every time.

## LONG PRAYERS

I remember shortly after I got saved that we were in church on a Wednesday evening and the Pastor asked a man to lead us in Prayer. This man stood up and prayed one of the longest, loudest and most powerful prayers I have ever heard. I was very impressed. I thought to myself, I need to learn how to pray like that.

I thought about that prayer for weeks, until I heard that the man lived out in the woods, in a small trailer with his wife and eight children. They were broke and sick most of the time and depended on hand outs to survive. I quickly realized that although prayers can sometimes be long, loud and powerful, that is not what causes them to be answered.

I have also known other people who were considered to be "Great Prayer Warriors" and they never got any results either. It's not a matter of how long and loud the prayer is, it's a matter of the faith of the person doing the praying.

## PRAYER GROUPS

Prayer groups are usually not effective, but many people like the idea of belonging to a prayer group. I think they like the social aspect of praying with friends and being close to likeminded people and that is always a good thing. Most of the time when people pray in "Prayer meetings" they do not really expect to see any results and so they do not get any, but they sure enjoy being there.

I do not pray with groups although I get invitations all the time to participate. I am honest and usually just say "I do not pray with groups but if you need something from God, I will get it for you."

The simple truth is this, when I pray, I mean business.

I will however, praise God with groups which we love to do. If you want to play some music and just praise God, count me in.

## PRAYER CHAINS

Churches mostly use prayer chains to keep people connected to each other and give people a common goal. I have never personally known of anyone who got a healing or financial miracle, or who even got saved because the prayer chain was activated in their behalf. One lady said to me, not so long ago, "I have four prayer chains praying for us." I thought to myself, that is not enough.

On Facebook, when people get sick they post, "Prayers needed." Other people then post in the comment section, "Prayers going up." I am thinking to myself, this person needs help.

## PRAYER ALONE DOES NOT SAVE PEOPLE

Years ago, I got a call from one of the elders of the church that Mary and I were attending. She said that the church was activating people to pray for a man who was dying in one of the nursing homes in town. He had been completely paralyzed on his left side for six months, due to a stroke. He had not eaten any food for three weeks, had nothing to drink for over a week and was, according to her, almost dead and not saved.

I said, "Who is going over there to see him?' She said, "No one, we are just praying for his salvation." I said, "That will not help him. Stop praying for him, pray for me and I will go see him." She said, "I never heard of such a thing." She then abruptly hung up the phone.

That evening I went to see the "Dying man." He was, just as the lady had said, almost dead. He received Jesus as his Savior and was also completely healed. Three months later he walked his daughter down the aisle at her wedding. Glory to God!

Prayer alone does not save anyone. Someone must tell them about Jesus and lead them in the prayer of salvation.

## YOU CAN BARGAIN WITH GOD

Moses talked God out of destroying the children of Israel, when they had sinned by making the golden calf.

> **Exodus 32:10-14 therefore let me alone, that my wrath may wax hot against them, and that I may consume them: and I will make of thee a great nation.**

**11 And Moses besought the LORD his God, and said, LORD, why do You wrath hot against thy people, which thou hast brought forth out of the land of Egypt with great power, and with a mighty hand?**

**12 Wherefore should the Egyptians speak, and say, for mischief did he bring them out, to slay them in the mountains, and to consume them from the face of the earth? Turn from thy fierce wrath, and repent of this evil against thy people.**

**13 Remember Abraham, Isaac, and Israel, thy servants, to whom thou swore by thine own self, and said unto them, I will multiply your seed as the stars of heaven, and all this land that I have spoken of will I give unto your seed, and they shall inherit it forever.**

**14 And the LORD repented of the evil which he thought to do unto his people.**

Because Israel sinned, by making the golden calf to be their idol, God decided to destroy the entire nation and start over again with Moses. Moses pleaded his case by reminding God of His covenant with Abraham, Isaac and Jacob and also by giving Him other reasons why He shouldn't destroy all the people and God changed His mind.

## DAVID MADE A DEAL WITH GOD.

**Psalm 51:9-13 Hide thy face from my sins, and blot out all mine iniquities.**

**10 Create in me a clean heart, O God; and renew a right spirit within me.**

**11 Cast me not away from thy presence; and take not thy holy spirit from me.**

**12 Restore unto me the joy of thy salvation; and uphold me with thy free spirit.**

**13 Then will I teach transgressors thy ways; and sinners shall be converted unto thee.**

This happened after King David had sinned. Here he asked God's forgiveness and then makes a deal that if God will forgive him he will tell people about Him.

## JACOB MADE A DEAL WITH GOD.

**Genesis 28:20-22 And Jacob vowed a vow, saying, If God will be with me, and will keep me in this way that I go, and will give me bread to eat, and raiment to put on,**

**21 So that I come again to my father's house in peace; then shall the LORD be my God:**

**22 And this stone, which I have set for a pillar, shall be God's house: and of all that thou shalt give me I will surely give the tenth unto thee.**

Jacob tells God that if He will protect him, provide food for him, give him clothes to wear and bring him home safely, then he will serve Him. He also vows to give God 10% of everything that He gives him. What Jacob did still works today.

## MY DEAL WITH GOD

I made a deal with God the day I got saved. I said, "Lord, if You will forgive me and accept me, I will serve

You the rest of my life." He did forgive me and accept me and I intend to keep my end of the bargain.

Five Years ago, Mary and I made another deal with God, a vow to tithe, like Jacob had done. I said, Lord, I will give you 10% of everything you give me. We are now living in abundance.

## HEZEKIAH CHANGED GOD'S MIND

**Isaiah 38:1-5 In those days was Hezekiah sick unto death. And Isaiah the prophet the son of Amoz came unto him, and said unto him, thus says the LORD, set thine house in order: for thou shalt die, and not live.**

**2 Then Hezekiah turned his face toward the wall, and prayed unto the LORD,**

**3 And said, remember now, O LORD, I beseech thee, how I have walked before thee in truth and with a perfect heart, and have done that which is good in thy sight. And Hezekiah wept sore.**

**[4] Then came the word of the LORD to Isaiah, saying,**

**[5] Go, and say to Hezekiah, thus says the LORD, the God of David thy father, I have heard thy prayer, I have seen thy tears: behold, I will add unto thy days fifteen years.**

Hezekiah was able to live an additional 15 years because he reminded God of what a good person he was. If things are not going well for you maybe you should remind God of who you are. I remind God every night that I am a covenant person and because of that, He should BLESS me and give me favor.

## CHANGE THE WAY YOU PRAY

Most people will pray the same way for years, even though they are not getting their prayers answered. If what you are doing is not working, do something different.

David asked God, in 2 Samuel 21:1 what was wrong, because his prayer about the famine was not being answered. God told him what the problem was. David fixed it and Israel had rain. How simple is that?

# HOW TO APPROACH GOD

## BOLDLY

Hebrews 4:16 Let us therefore come boldly unto the throne of grace, that we may obtain mercy, and find grace to help in time of need.

## THEN
## FROM A POSITION OF RIGHTEOUSNESS

2 Corinthians 5:21 For he hath made him to be sin for us, who knew no sin; that we might be made the righteousness of God in him.

Righteousness is actually "Right standing with God' and is a free gift.

Most people, including believers, have terrible feelings of guilt about their past and guilt will hinder your prayers.

Understanding righteousness will give you the ability to boldly come unto the Throne of Grace and stand in the presence of God without any sense of condemnation, shame, inferiority or guilt.

Approach God as a Child Approaches a Loving, Approving Father. You are God's child, He loves you and you belong at the Throne of Grace.

You will have much more success in your prayer life if you know who you are and understand your relationship with God.

## FREE FROM SIN

**1 John 1:9 If we confess our sins, he is faithful and just to forgive us our sins, and to cleanse us from all unrighteousness.**

If God has forgiven you of your sins and cleansed you from all unrighteousness, what does that make you? Righteous, of course. If you have repented of your sins you are automatically the righteousness of God by Christ Jesus.

> **Isaiah 43:25 I, even I, am he that blots out thy transgressions for mine own sake, and will not remember thy sins.**

God causes Himself to forget about your past sins, so when you pray, you should not be thinking, or talking about them any longer.

Several years ago, a man came up to me after church and said, "Pastor Jim, I now realize that I have a right to have my prayers answered." He had just received a revelation of righteousness.

Understanding Righteousness will cause you to realize that as a covenant person, you have a Blood bought, God given right to have your prayers answered. When this becomes a reality in your heart, your prayer life changes.

## WITH THANKSGIVING

**Philippians 4:6-7 Be careful for nothing; but in everything by prayer and supplication with thanksgiving let your requests be made known unto God.**

**[7] And the peace of God, which passes all understanding, shall keep your hearts and minds through Christ Jesus.**

I always start out by thanking God for this day. God has emotions, just like we do and He loves a heart filled with gratitude for what He has done for us.

# WHAT NOT TO PRAY ABOUT

We are not supposed to pray about everything. There are actually many things we should not be praying about.

## PROBLEMS OR OBSTACLES

> **Mark 11:23 For verily I say unto you, that whosoever shall say unto this mountain, be thou removed, and be thou cast into the sea; and shall not doubt in his heart, but shall believe that those things which he says shall come to pass; he shall have whatsoever he says.**

The mountain in this verse is any problem or obstacle hindering you from living an abundant life. Obstacles and problems are not to be prayed about, they are to be spoken to. Tell them to leave you in the Name of Jesus and they will.

## STORMS OF LIFE

Storms of life can come in many forms and none of them are to be prayed about. Jesus is our example.

> **Mark 4:35-41 And the same day, when the evening was come, he said unto them, let us pass over unto the other side.**
>
> **36 And when they had sent away the multitude, they took him even as he was in the ship. And there were also with him other little ships.**
>
> **37 And there arose a great storm of wind, and the waves beat into the ship, so that it was now full.**
>
> **38 And he was in the back part of the ship, asleep on a pillow: and they woke him, and**

**said unto him, Master, don't you care that we perish?**

**39 And he arose, and rebuked the wind, and said unto the sea, Peace, be still. And the wind ceased, and there was a great calm.**

**40 And he said unto them, why are ye so fearful? how is it that ye have no faith?**

**41 And they feared exceedingly, and said one to another, what manner of man is this, that even the wind and the sea obey him?**

Jesus did not pray about this storm. Instead, He spoke to the storm and told it to stop. You should not pray about any storm that arises in your life. You should do exactly what Jesus did. Instead of praying about storms, speak to them and tell them to stop. Or have your Pastor or Teaching Minister do it for you.

I have spent much of my life, as many of you have, fighting my way through one storm after another. Never again will I fight my way through a storm, such as sickness or strife or fear or stress or anything bad. I just tell it to leave in the Name of Jesus and it leaves. I also calm storms in the lives of people in my church and my partners on a daily basis.

## SICKNESS

**Luke 13:10-13 And Jesus was teaching in one of the synagogues on the sabbath.**

**11 And, behold, there was a woman which had a spirit of infirmity eighteen years, and was bowed together, and could in no wise lift up herself.**

**12 And when Jesus saw her, he called her to him, and said unto her, Woman, thou art loosed from thine infirmity.**

**13 And he laid his hands on her: and immediately she was made straight, and glorified God.**

Jesus never prayed for a sick person and neither do I and I have seen thousands of people healed through our healing ministry. I do what Jesus did in Luke Chapter

13. Step one, Jesus told the spirit of infirmity, which had bound her for 18 years, to leave. Step two, Jesus laid His Hand on her and she straightened up and was healed.

Jesus did not deal with sick people, He dealt with the spirit of infirmity that was causing the sickness, and so do I.

Much of sickness and disease is what the doctors call hereditary, which is actually generational curses of sickness. Cancer, heart disease, diabetes, high blood pressure, just to name a few of them. There are many more. When I break the generational curses of sickness and disease, people get healed.

## POVERTY

> **Deuteronomy 28:29 And thou shalt grope at noonday, as the blind gropes in darkness, and thou shalt not prosper in thy ways: and thou shalt be only oppressed and spoiled forever, and no man shall save thee.**

This verse shows us the reason for poverty. The curse of the law and generational curses of poverty are handed down through families. Almost all poor people come from poor families. Generational curses of poverty can run in families for hundreds of years. People would say poverty is hereditary when actually it is a generational curse.

## FIND SOMEONE TO HELP YOU

When people, who are struggling financially, either come into my church or call me, the first thing I do is break the curse of the law and the generational curse of poverty in their life, in the Name of Jesus. I then speak THE BLESSING OF ABRAHAM over them and speak to their finances and tell them to increase in the Name of Jesus. This allows THE BLESSING OF GOD to begin operating and within 6 months to a year their lives change as THE BLESSING grows. You would be amazed by how this works. I do this with people in my church and my partners. The list of Praise Reports is huge.

# THE PRAYER OF FAITH

**James 5:15-16 is anyone sick among you? let him call for the elders of the church; and let them pray over him, anointing him with oil in the name of the Lord:**

**15 And the prayer of faith shall save the sick, and the Lord shall raise him up; and if he has committed sins, they shall be forgiven him.**

The prayer of faith is actually the **Only Prayer** that God will ever answer. God will not answer any prayer, no matter what you are praying for, unless it is a prayer of faith.

There is always a reason when prayers are not answered and unanswered prayer is never God's fault.

**Hebrews 11:6 But without faith it is impossible to please God: for he that cometh to God must believe that he is, and that he is a rewarder of them that diligently seek him.**

This verse actually means that without faith, you will get nothing from God.

The simple definition of the prayer of faith is that it is a prayer where the person doing the praying absolutely expects God to give them what they ask for, with no doubt.

## ACCORDING TO YOUR FAITH

**Matthew 9:29 Jesus said, according to your faith be it unto you**

We receive everything we get from God according to faith.

Faith to get your prayers answered begins where the will of God is known. Find the scripture that promises what you want or need and that is where you should base your faith.

My faith to pray for anything is always based on scripture. Some examples are:

- Healing: 1 Peter 2:24
- Needs: Philippians 4:19
- Forgiveness: 1 John 1:9
- Abundance: John 10:10
- THE BLESSING: Galatians 3:29

## GOD'S TIMING

When prayers have not been answered, many people will sigh and say, "Well, God's timing is perfect." This is just an excuse for unanswered prayers. People who wait on God's timing never seem to get any prayers answered.

For some reason God's timing always coincides with your faith because according to what Jesus said in Matthew 9:29 we receive according to our faith.

Two questions: Does God make people wait when they pray the prayer of salvation? Does God make people wait when they ask Him for forgiveness? The answer to both of these questions is of course, no. Well then why are so many people willing to wait for healing and provision?

If your prayer has not been answered there is a problem and the problem is always a faith problem. Correct it, and you will get answers.

## THE LAW OF FAITH

> **Romans 3:27 Where is boasting then? It is excluded. By what law? of works? Nay: but by the law of faith.**

The law of faith also applies to prayer. In order for any prayer to get answered, someone involved in that prayer must have faith.

If God answered any prayer, other than the prayer of faith, He would be breaking His own law of faith, which He will never do.

The prayer of faith will not only heal the sick but will save your soul, pay your bills and get you anything else you need or want from God.

## HOW FAITH COMES

**Romans 10:17 So then faith comes by hearing the Word of God.**

The more of God's Word you hear, the stronger your faith will be and the easier it will be for you to get your prayers answered. The easiest way to hear God's Word is to read your Bible out loud.

A lady said to me, several years ago at a conference, "Pastor Jim, I have been praying all day for God to increase my faith." I said, "Well, you have been wasting your time and God's." God will not increase your faith. That is up to you and you do it by hearing His Word.

## INCREASING MY FAITH

Several years ago, I called Mary into the office and said, "I know why we are struggling with our finances."

She responded, "Why is that?" I said, "Because I don't have enough faith." She replied, "Well get the faith" turned around and walked away. I yelled back to her, "I will."

I was determined not to stay broke because I knew that God's people are not supposed to live in poverty or lack. I started feeding my spirit on God's Word concerning finances. I did this for hours every day. Day after day, week after week, month after month and year after year. Now we live in abundance. God's Word works! My determination factor was very high. How high is yours?

You do not have to wait as long for abundance because we have discovered shortcuts which we share with our church and partners. It is usually not an overnight process, but we have cut down the time considerably that it takes for THE BLESSING OF GOD to take effect in people's lives.

## EXPECT MORE THAN YOU ASK FOR

**Ephesians 3:20 Now unto him that is able to do exceeding abundantly above all that**

**we ask or think, according to the power that worketh in us.**

I used to be surprised when God would give me more than I asked for but now I expect it because God is so wonderful and loves us more than we can ever imagine.

## THE FORMULA FOR ANSWERED PRAYER

**Mark 11:24 Therefore I say unto you, what things so ever you desire, when you pray, believe that you receive them, and you shall have them.**

Many people hope they will receive when they pray. However, in this verse Jesus is telling us that we can have absolutely anything we desire when we pray, if we can believe we receive, not hope we receive. If you are hoping you receive, you will never get it. Many people say that seeing is believing, but with God, first you believe and then you see it. This is not as difficult as you might think.

**Mark 9:23 Jesus said, if you can believe, all things are possible to him who believes.**

Here Jesus is telling us that we have no limitations on our life if we have faith. When I got a revelation of this verse, years ago, it changed my life. I began to live, talk, think and act like there is nothing I can't do, nothing I can't have and nothing I can't be. All I have to do is just increase my faith for it by hearing God's Word over and over.

**Galatians 3:28 There is neither Jew nor Greek, there is neither bond nor free, there is neither male nor female: for you are all the same in Christ Jesus.**

It doesn't matter who you are, where you came from, what your background is, how old or young you are, nothing is impossible for you if you can believe.

## ASKING IN FAITH

**James 1:5-8 If any of you lack wisdom, let him ask of God, that giveth to all men liberally, and upbraids not; and it shall be given him.**

**6 But let him ask in faith, nothing wavering. For he that wavers is like a wave of the sea driven with the wind and tossed.**

**[7] For let not that man think that he shall receive any thing of the Lord.**

**[8] A double minded man is unstable in all his ways.**

This verse is referring to asking God for wisdom. However, you could substitute absolutely anything else in this prayer besides wisdom, because this simple formula pertains to asking God for everything else as well. The word wavering means doubting. We must ask in faith, with no doubt.

## REMOVING DOUBT

Doubt is the prayer and BLESSING blocker. Doubt on your part, will always prevent God from answering your prayers.

The word doubt means double minded, considering two outcomes. Maybe God will answer my prayer, or maybe God won't. Maybe I will get healed, or maybe I will die. Maybe I will have enough money to pay my bills, or maybe I won't. You get the point.

**Romans 4:19-21 And being not weak in faith, Abraham stopped considering his own body now dead, when he was about a hundred years old, and did not consider the deadness of Sarah's womb when she was ninety years old.**

**[20] He doubted not at the promise of God through unbelief; but was strong in faith, giving glory to God;**

**[21] And being fully persuaded that, what God had promised, He was able also to perform.**

It took Abraham 24 years to stop doubting what God had promised about him and Sarah having a baby in their old age. Finally, Abraham and Sarah got to the point where they refused to consider their old bodies and just believed what God had told them. When the doubt was gone, they had a baby while Abraham was 100 years old and Sarah was 90.

**Hebrews 11:11 Through faith also Sara herself received strength to conceive seed, and was delivered of a child when she was past**

**age, because she judged God faithful to what He had promised.**

## REFUSING TO DOUBT IS A DECISION

The way to remove doubt, is to make a decision to absolutely refuse to consider anything other than God's Word, regarding your situation or circumstances. You do this, and you will find yourself getting your prayers answered on a regular basis.

Never Pray, "If it be thy will." That is the doubt creator. You are expected to know God's will before you pray. His will for everything, pertaining to your life, is in the Bible.

## STOP PRAYING

To ask God again, after you have prayed and asked God for something, is a sure sign that you do not believe you have received. People who keep asking after I have prayed for them never seem to receive. **It nullifies the prayer.**

**Matthew 6:7 But when you pray, use not vain repetitions, as the heathen do: for they think that they shall be heard for their much speaking.**

If you pray and believe that you receive, why would you ask God for the same thing tomorrow? The only reason you would, is because you did not really believe you received the first time.

If I pray for someone and then they go ask someone else to also pray for them, I tell them to stay with the other person. I know they will not receive.

I sometimes ask people this question. If Jesus Himself prayed for you, or spoke over you concerning something, would you go home and keep asking God for it or would you believe it was a done deal? Then why do you keep asking God, after I have prayed for you?

The people who keep praying and fussing and asking, "When am I going to see something" are the ones who never get it.

It has been my experience that the people whom I have BLESSED, ministered to for healing, or prayed for about other things, and then have gone about their business and not even been concerned about it, have been the ones who received what they need.

So many times, we have had people brought into our church, terminally ill with cancer who were ministered to and did not even know what was going on. All they knew was that I prayed for them and they didn't think much about it. They start feeling better very quickly, went back to the doctor two weeks later and there was no sign of cancer.

## STOP TALKING

> **Proverbs 3:5 Trust in the LORD with all thine heart; and lean not unto thine own understanding.**

You are not called by God to understand all of this. I certainly don't. You are just called to believe it. I don't understand everything about this computer I am using, but I can use it. I tell people this, the more you try to understand this, the more you talk about this and the more questions you ask, the longer it takes.

**Psalm 141:3 Set a watch, O Lord, over my mouth; keep the door of my lips.**

That is why I keep a roll of duct tape by my pulpit at all times. If I could put a piece of duct tape over your mouth right after I pray for you, in less than six months, you would be healed and rich. You can use spiritual duct tape.

## FAITH IN THE NAME OF JESUS

**Mark 16:17 And these signs shall follow them that have faith in My Name.**

The word "Signs" means miracles. Faith in the Name of Jesus will get your prayers answered also.

**John 16:23 And in that day, you shall ask me nothing. Verily, verily, I say unto you, whatsoever you shall ask the Father in my name, he will give it you.**

**Faith in the Name of Jesus is the Key to getting every prayer answered.**

Everyone uses that Wonderful Name, but only people who have a very high level of faith in That Name will get results.

When you have faith in The Name of Jesus, your prayers will be answered because of the power in that Name.

Very simply, I just believe that when I use The Name of Jesus, my prayers are going to be answered every single time and they are!

## UNFORGIVENESS

**Mark 11:25 And when you stand praying, forgive, if you are holding grudges against anyone: that your Father also which is in heaven may forgive you your trespasses.**

Faith, to get prayers answered, will not work in an unforgiving heart.

## HONOR YOUR WIFE

**1 Peter 3:7 Likewise, ye husbands, dwell with them according to knowledge, giving honor unto the wife, as unto the weaker vessel, and as being heirs together of the grace of life; that your prayers be not hindered.**

Always show your wife honor, or God will not answer your prayers.

## DEMANDING PRAYERS

This is done by Praying God's Word back to Him and demanding that He perform His Word. "Lord, Your Word says, now let's go." The promise of God is always the answer to your problem. Find it, consider it, meditate on it, speak it and demand it, until faith comes.

## DEMAND HEALING

I woke up at 7 AM on a Saturday morning with a kidney stone which was very painful. I was making spaghetti sauce for a dinner party that evening. The pain soon became excruciating. I said, “Lord, Your Word says that I was healed by the stripes of Jesus now You heal me.” Nothing happened, so I said it again. Again, nothing happened, so I said it again and this time louder. Still nothing. So, I kept saying it and the more I said it the louder I got. I finally said, very loud, “Lord, Your Word says that I was healed by the Strips of Jesus, now you heal me.”

It got so loud that Mary left the house. I kept going, louder and louder. Finally, at exactly 2 PM God spoke to me in an audible voice and said, I am going to heal you. Go to the party tonight and there will be a woman there. He showed me a picture of her in my mind. Have her pray for you and I will heal you. It happened just like God had said it would, and I was healed.

The next time you are sick say the same thing 1,000 times loudly, and watch what happens. You might say

"Pastor Jim, that takes a lot of time." I ask, "How badly do you want to get healed of cancer or heart disease or whatever sickness you may have?" What is your determination factor to receive your healing?

## DEMAND FINANCIAL INCREASE

Lord, You said, in **Proverbs 3:9-10** that if I honor You by bringing the first fruits of all my increase to You that You would fill my barns. (My bank account) Now let's go!

These two verses provided for us while we were in Bible College. We had run out of money and I read this passage on a Thursday morning and started praying the verses back to God. The more I did it, the louder I got. Our finances broke open that same afternoon, and we had plenty of money for our time at Bible College. We even had enough money to help other students.

Lord, Your Word says in **2 Corinthians 8:9** that Jesus became poor so that I could become rich, now You make me rich. (Rich means more than enough money to pay my bills)

Lord, you said, in **Malachi 3:10** that if I bring my tithe to you I should test You and now I am. Now You open the windows of Heaven like You said You would and pour me out a Blessing that I do not have enough room to receive.

Keep praying these verses back to God and demand that He perform them in your life. If you do this long enough, at some point your faith will climb to the level that it takes to get what you want or need. This absolutely works every time if your determination factor is high enough and you don't quit.

## REMIND GOD

> **Isaiah 43:26 Put me in remembrance: let us plead together: declare thou, that thou may be justified.**

This is what demanding prayers are. Reminding God of what His Word says and demanding that He perform it. The promises of God are the answers to your prayers and God delights when His children have the audacity to say "Lord, You promised it, so now do it."

After you pray, it is certainly OK to keep reminding God what His Word says about your situation or circumstances. Doing this will strengthen your faith and the more you do it, the stronger your faith will get.

## PRAY WITH INSISTENCE

**Luke 11:8 I say unto you, although he will not rise and give him food, just because he is his friend, yet because of his importunity (Insistence or persistence) he will rise and give him as much food as he needs.**

The more insistent, or persistent, your prayer is, the more likely it will be answered. Never be ready to settle for not having your prayers answered. Insist that your prayers be answered. Be persistent and you will get results.

## SEND GOD'S WORD BACK TO HIM

**Isaiah 55:11 so shall my word be that goes forth out of my mouth: it shall not return**

> **unto me void, but it shall accomplish that which I please, and it shall prosper in the thing whereto I sent it.**

When you remind God, by praying His Word back to him, you are actually sending it back to Him. Since God's Word will not return to Him void, but will accomplish that which He originally sent it to do, guess what is going to happen. Keep sending God's Word back to Him until it manifests in your life.

I sent God's Word, concerning THE BLESSING, back to Him every day, all day long, for eight months. I kept saying, "Lord, Your Word says that THE BLESSING of Abraham is my inheritance, now You BLESS ME."

Finally, God actually spoke to me in an audible voice, inside my belly, and told me what to do to receive THE BLESSING. I did what He said to do and now we live in abundance. You do not need to go through all that because now that we know how to get THE BLESSING, we share it with our church and partners and everyone. I know how to get THE BLESSING to come upon someone, even you, very quickly.

Truth of the matter is, many people know about THE BLESSING OF ABRAHAM, but <u>very few people</u> actually know how to get it to come upon themselves or someone else. I know how to do this!

When you speak God's Word back to him, the first person to hear it is you, because your ear is only 4 inches from your mouth. Since faith comes by hearing God's Word, your faith is going to grow. You can only hear something a certain number of times before you believe it and when you believe it, you get it.

> **John 14:13 And whatsoever you shall ask in my name, that will I do, that the Father may be glorified in the Son.**

The words **<u>shall ask</u>** in this verse, in the original Greek, actually means demand as something due. This verse should have been translated, whatsoever you shall demand, as something due you, in my Name, that will I do. The promises of God are all something due you and you have a right to have them in the Name of Jesus.

Decide what you need, find the promise pertaining to your need, ask God for it and then pray that scripture back to God out loud, demanding that it manifest in your life. This works every time if you are persistent and do not quit.

# PRAYER OF AGREEMENT

**Matthew 18:19 Again I say unto you, that if two of you shall agree on earth as touching anything that they shall ask, it shall be done for them of my Father which is in heaven.**

The prayer of agreement is when two people agree in prayer, or become united together, in asking God for something. Like any other prayer, faith must be involved. The truth of the matter is, that only **<u>one</u>** of the two people agreeing in prayer needs to have faith in order for the prayer to be answered.

God is so wonderful, that He has made a way for people with little or no faith to get healed, to receive THE BLESSING, and to have their prayers answered.

## MY PRAYER MINISTRY

I have a wonderful prayer ministry which is based entirely upon the prayer of agreement. I spend most of my day praying with people over the phone. These are people who do not have a Pastor available who can help them get their prayers answered. We have amazing results. Everyone needs a **Personal Pastor** who has faith to get prayers answered.

## GIVING FAITH A BOOST

The prayer of agreement is like jumper cables stretched between the batteries of two cars. The stronger battery will help the weaker battery start the car. That is exactly how the prayer of agreement works. When two people agree in prayer, the person with the stronger faith will help the person with the weaker faith get their prayer answered.

I have to give credit about the jumper cables to John Thomas, from our church, who came up with this one Sunday morning after church. When he said it, I said, "Whoa, that is exactly how the prayer of agreement works."

I tell people who are sick or broke that I am going to agree with them in prayer, combine my faith with theirs and give their faith a boost. I have prayed with and spoken over some great and famous men and woman of God, even healing evangelists who's faith just needed a boost, and they were able to receive their healing.

Be quick to ask for help if you need it. I have heard people say "If I can't get it by my own faith, I don't want it." That is pride and pride is terrible and ugly and will lead to destruction. I am very quick to ask for help if I am not receiving what I want or need from God. I always say that when I want or need something from God, "I don't care whose faith I have to use to get it!"

## HANNAH AND ELI THE PRIEST

**1 Samuel 1:17 Then Eli answered and said, go in peace: and the God of Israel grant thee thy petition that thou hast asked of him.**

Hannah was barren, could not have a child and was, at this point, even past the age of having children. Eli, the Priest, agreed with her when he stated that God would grant her request. She knew that when Eli had spoken, it was done. According to **1 Samuel 1:18** her countenance was no longer sad. She soon had a son and named him Samuel.

## CHECK YOUR FAITH

> **2 Corinthians 13:5 Examine yourselves, whether you be in the faith; prove your own selves.**

This verse is telling us to examine ourselves to see if our faith is strong enough to receive what we need from God. Actually, we should always do this before we pray about anything.

If you are not getting your prayers answered, it is probably because your faith level is not high enough in that area. If that is the case, find someone who has the faith for what you want or need and who will agree with you in prayer, and you will receive an answer every time.

Make sure that the person agreeing with you has strong faith or you will get no results.

## FIND SOMEONE WITH FAITH

You do not need to activate the prayer chain, or have a large number of people pray for you. All you need is one person who can pray the prayer of faith, in agreement with you, to get your prayers answered. How easy is that?

This is how my prayer ministry works and why so many people who call me get their prayer requests granted by God. I take being asked to agree with someone in prayer very seriously. I tell people, when they ask me to agree with them in prayer, "The answer to your prayer is now my responsibility, let me have this."

## MY FAITH IS AVAILABLE

People call me all the time and say, "Pastor Jim, I need to use your faith." I tell them "Ok, you can use my faith for this and then you can use your faith to help someone else." Many people can use their faith to help other people with their needs, but they need a boast to get their own needs met. And that is OK.

The prayer of agreement is how I use my faith to get the prayers of other people answered.

Peter did this in **Acts Chapter 3.** The man at the Temple gate had absolutely no faith for healing. Peter however, had faith in the Name of Jesus and according to verse 16, that is what caused this man to be healed.

**1 Kings 17:9-16** Elijah used his faith to help the widow woman and her household have enough food to eat.

**2 Kings 4:1-7** Elisha used his faith to help a widow pay off her debt, so that her sons would not be taken away from her.

In my prayer ministry, I use my faith every day, to help people get healed, receive THE BLESSING and get their prayers answered.

We have literally had thousands of people get their prayers answered and get healed through the prayer of agreement. Many of them had little or no faith for what they want or need, but I have faith in The Name of Jesus. That is why people get healed and prayers get answered. I am also quick to say, I am not the only one who can do this.

If you need help, find someone who operates on the same level of faith that Peter did in the book of Acts. They will agree with you in prayer and you will soon get your prayers answered.

# ABOUT THE AUTHOR

Pastor Jim Kibler was born in Pittsburgh and grew up in Slippery Rock, Pennsylvania. He is a graduate of Mount St. Mary's College in Emmitsburg, Maryland and Rhema Bible College in Tulsa, Oklahoma. He also did graduate work in business at George Washington University in Washington DC.

Pastor Jim and his wife Mary, also a graduate of Rhema Bible College, Pastor Life Church in Indialantic, Florida. Their church is across the river from Melbourne.

Pastor Jim's popular website is www.increasenow.com, a **FREE SITE**, where people around the world watch his FREE 15 Minute videos every day, on God's

Goodness, Prayer, Healing, Redemption, Abundance and The Blessing.

Also watch Pastor Jim's live broadcast every day by downloading the free Periscope App on your phone and follow Pastor Jim Kibler

## FOLLOW PASTOR JIM KIBLER ON FACEBOOK AND INSTAGRAM

In addition, Pastor Jim is a Very Entertaining Conference Speaker. Everywhere he speaks, people get healed, finances increase and churches grow. He makes God's Word very easy to understand. He also has a very anointed healing ministry with people being healed of all types of diseases and blind eyes opened.

Pastor Jim has a wonderful Prayer Ministry and he makes himself available to pray with people who do not have a Pastor to pray with them. He is **Personal Pastor** to many people who otherwise do not have a Pastor to talk to, Speak THE BLESSING over them, or Pray the Prayer of AGREEMENT for their needs.

His Prayer Ministry has had incredible results. People getting prayers answered every day. Many people are healed right over the phone and have THE BLESSING OF ABRAHAM activated in their lives.

Pastor Jim's phone number is available at www.increasenow.com. You can also sign up to be notified about FREE books and videos.

He is called the **"How To Preacher"** because he not only teaches people what God has promised, but how to receive it.

This book, "How To Pray" is available at Amazon. Tell Everyone.

Other Books by Pastor Jim:

The Blessing (Available at Amazon)

Jesus (Available at Amazon)

If the Bible Is True (Available through the website)

88842524R00039

Made in the USA
Columbia, SC
09 February 2018